HOW THE GOVERNMENT WORKS

BY JEANNE MARIE FORD

Published by The Child's World®
1980 Lookout Drive • Mankato, MN 56003-1705
800-599-READ • www.childsworld.com

ACKNOWLEDGMENTS
The Child's World®: Mary Swensen, Publishing Director
Red Line Editorial: Editorial direction and production
The Design Lab: Design

Photographs ©: Phil Sears/AP Images, cover, 2; iStockphoto, 5,
14; Claudio Divizia/Shutterstock Images, 6; Michael Reynolds/
EPA/Corbis, 10; Natalia Bratslavsky/Shutterstock Images,
11; Shutterstock Images, 12 (top), 12 (bottom); Asia Glab/
Shutterstock Images, 12 (middle); Red Line Editorial, 16; Steve
Cannon/AP Images, 17; Will & Deni McIntyre/Corbis, 18; Eric
Broder Van Dyke/Shutterstock Images, 20; Albin Lohr-Jones/
Sipa/AP Images, 21

ISBN 9781503809048
LCCN 2015958458

Printed in the United States of America
Mankato, MN
June, 2016
PA02309

**On the cover: Members of the Florida House of
Representatives meet for a session.**

TABLE OF CONTENTS

CHAPTER 1

FORMING THE U.S. GOVERNMENT

overnments have important responsibilities. They create and enforce laws. They decide what to do when people break the laws. They provide services, such as education. Good governments protect people from dangers.

There are many different types of governments. The United States is a **democracy**. In a democracy, people vote for their leaders. They can also run for office themselves. The United States was one of the first democracies. Yet the nation's founders followed examples from other places, too.

In ancient Greece, people practiced an early form of democracy. **Citizens** held meetings to vote on important decisions. The meetings were not open to everyone. Only male citizens 18 years old or older could vote. The meetings gave these citizens a say in their communities. Eventually, the system changed. There were too many people to hold meetings. **Representatives** were chosen to carry out the people's will.

In ancient Greece, citizens discussed and voted
on important issues.

The United States began as 13 British colonies. Britain
was ruled by a king. Britain also had a **parliament**. Some
members were elected by their communities. Members of
the parliament could vote on important decisions. The king
needed their approval on many issues.

Britain set rules for the American colonists. Colonists had
no representatives in the government. Over time, colonists
grew frustrated with the king and the parliament. Rebel

The British Parliament has met at
Westminster Palace for hundreds of years.

colonists wanted to be free. In 1776, these colonists decided to form their own nation.

The rebelling colonists declared that they were free from British rule. But they had to fight a war to win their freedom. In 1783, the colonists won the war. The United States was officially a free nation.

Americans needed to set up a government. In 1777, the colonies adopted the Articles of Confederation. This was the nation's first **constitution**. It made the 13 colonies into states. It also created a weak national government. The government could not tax people. It had no way of paying for services. There was no president. The states had most of the power.

Problems with this system soon became clear. The states had different needs and populations. Each state wanted its own powers. To stay together as one nation, the country needed a new plan.

In 1787, the founders wrote the U.S. Constitution. This document granted power to both the **federal** government and the states. This sharing of power is called **federalism**. A president would lead the nation. Citizens would vote for their president. States would also have representatives.

These officials would serve in the national government. In addition, states could develop their own laws. Each state could develop its own system of local governments. These would serve counties, cities, and towns.

In creating a government, the founders used ideas from other places. They drew on ancient Greek ideas about democracy. Like the British, they formed a **legislature** with two chambers or parts. In many ways, though, the U.S. system was new.

Today, our government is still based on the Constitution. National, state, and local governments have their own roles. They make and enforce laws. They also give us police, soldiers, and teachers. They maintain roads, schools, and libraries. Government workers print our money. They deliver our mail. Most of us use government services every day of our lives.

U.S. TERRITORIES

There are some U.S. lands that are not states. These are known as territories. Many are islands where no one lives. But five U.S. territories have residents. These include Guam and Puerto Rico. People who live in these places have many of the rights of other U.S. residents. However, they cannot vote in federal elections. They do not have representatives in the federal government.

CHAPTER 2

THE FEDERAL GOVERNMENT

The nation's founders laid out a plan for the federal government. We still use this plan today. The federal government has three branches. Each branch has its own responsibilities. The branches also work together. The legislative branch makes laws. The executive branch enforces the laws. The judicial branch interprets the laws. It decides how the laws should be applied.

The legislative branch contains the U.S. Congress. Congress has two parts. One is the House of Representatives. The other is the Senate. The Senate has 100 members. There are two members from each state. The House of Representatives has 435 members. The number of members from each state is based on state populations. States where more people live have more representatives than states where fewer people live.

Congress has the power to pass laws. It plans the national budget. It also has the power to declare war. People

Each year, members of Congress and other government officials gather to hear the president's State of the Union address.

vote for members of Congress. Each member represents a state or district.

The executive branch includes the president, vice president, and Cabinet. The Cabinet is made up of the president's **advisers**. Each adviser leads a different department. Some departments include the Department of Education and the Department of Transportation.

One of the president's duties is to command the military. The president also appoints federal judges. Often, he or she meets with leaders of other countries.

The judicial branch includes district courts, courts of appeals, and the U.S. Supreme Court.

The judicial branch is the court system. The system includes three types of courts. District courts make decisions in trials. Appeals courts sometimes review the district courts' decisions. Appeals courts are also known as higher courts. The highest court is the Supreme Court. It can review decisions from lower courts.

THREE BRANCHES OF GOVERNMENT

LEGISLATIVE BRANCH

Senate

House of Representatives

EXECUTIVE BRANCH

president

vice president

Cabinet

JUDICIAL BRANCH

Supreme Court — lower federal courts

The president appoints federal judges. The Senate then votes to approve or reject the judges. Often, these judges serve for life. The president also appoints people to the Supreme Court. The Court has nine judges. They are called justices.

TRIBAL GOVERNMENTS

For a long time, Native Americans did not have many rights. They were not considered U.S. citizens until 1924. Today, federal laws protect their rights. But many tribes also have their own governments. Each tribe is a "nation within a nation." Most tribes have an elected leader and council. Some also have tribal courts.

The government uses a system of checks and balances. Each branch reviews what the other branches do. The Supreme Court reviews laws passed by Congress. Justices can overturn or cancel laws that violate the Constitution. Congress votes on many of the president's decisions. It can reject appointed judges. The president reviews bills passed by Congress. The president can sign or **veto** a bill. Sometimes, Congress can work around the veto. If two-thirds of the members vote for the bill, they can override, or set aside, the veto. This system makes sure that no branch of government has too much power.

Some government workers are well-known. Presidents appear on television. Members of Congress speak publicly about what they do. Yet there are many other federal workers. The president's Cabinet has 15 departments. Each has a staff of workers. There are hundreds of government

Each year, people pay taxes to the Internal Revenue Service. The tax money pays for many services.

agencies, too. **Diplomats** work to keep peace with other nations. Military officers help keep the country safe. Scientists protect public health.

The federal government has many responsibilities. It protects forests and maintains national parks. It regulates banks, food, and medicine. It helps people who are sick. One agency is the Internal Revenue Service (IRS). The IRS collects taxes. These taxes pay for government services.

Over the years, the government has gotten bigger. In 1792, there were about 780 federal workers. Now there are more than 2 million. Some people say the government is too large. They say it has too much control. Others wish the government offered more services.

CHAPTER 3

STATE GOVERNMENTS

State governments are often similar to the federal government. Each has three branches. State executive branches are led by governors. A governor is like the president of a state. State executive branches also include agencies and departments.

CAN STATES LEAVE THE NATION?

In 1861, the Civil War began. Eleven states seceded from the Union. They formed their own nation. President Abraham Lincoln said this act was illegal. The Constitution does not mention secession. Experts disagree about whether it is allowed. In 1865, the Union won the war. The United States became one nation again.

Almost all state legislatures have two chambers or houses. One is usually called the state senate. The other chamber is sometimes called the state house of representatives. Some states call it the general assembly.

State courts rule on cases about state laws. Governors appoint some

STATES AND THE FEDERAL GOVERNMENT

State governments are often similar to the federal government.
They have many of the same parts.

PART OF GOVERNMENT	FEDERAL GOVERNMENT	STATE GOVERNMENTS
highest law	U.S. Constitution	state constitution
leader	president	governor
highest court	U.S. Supreme Court	state supreme court
legislature	Senate and House of Representatives	state senate and state house of representatives or general assembly

state judges. Other judges are elected by the people. State
judges have set terms. They do not usually serve for life.

States run programs to help residents. The states
need money for these programs. The funds come from
a few different places. Some money is from the federal
government. Some is from state taxes. Most states collect

Florida Governor Rick Scott (far right) met with the state legislature on the first day of their session, or year, in 2016.

taxes on residents' income. They also take a portion of money that people spend when they shop. This is called a sales tax.

The states must work with federal and local governments. They help maintain schools, roads, and libraries. Each state has its own police force. The state military is called the National Guard. States fund public colleges and parks. State officials **issue** driver's licenses. They issue birth certificates when babies are born. They run elections. States provide many important services.

States help fund local libraries and schools.

Sometimes, federal and state laws conflict. According to the Constitution, federal laws are more important. They apply in all 50 states. But the Constitution protects states' rights, too. It lists the powers of the federal government. Other powers belong to the states or to the people.

The United States is a large country. Some states are mainly rural. Others are mostly urban. The states have different industries. Their populations have different needs. The states help serve the needs of their residents. Local governments help serve their residents, too.

CHAPTER 4

LOCAL GOVERNMENTS

In early America, local governments were important. Britain ruled the colonies, but the king and parliament were far away. Some areas held their own town meetings. Colonists voted on key issues and rules. Today, some towns still hold meetings. Most have a more organized system, too.

GOVERNMENT IN WASHINGTON, DC

Washington, DC, is the U.S. capital. It is not part of any state. George Washington chose the site of the capital in 1790. Land was taken from Maryland and Virginia to form the new city. A city government enforces local laws. City residents pay federal taxes. They can vote for the U.S. president. However, they do not have representatives in Congress.

Most states are divided into counties. Others are divided into boroughs or parishes. Some states divide counties into townships. These areas might include a few towns. Many towns and cities also have their own governments.

The Constitution says nothing about local

Police officers in San Francisco, California, prepare to provide security for a city event.

governments. States establish them. The states decide which powers towns, cities, or counties can have. Most can collect taxes. This money is used to pay firefighters and police. Local authorities provide drinking water. City or county workers collect trash and maintain roads. In wintry weather, they remove snow. Most public schools and libraries are controlled by local governments.

Councils often govern counties. Mayors run most cities and towns. Their jobs vary widely. More than 8 million people live in New York City. The city mayor works with many other officials. By contrast, some towns only have a few thousand people. These town governments are very small. Some mayors have a lot of power. Others share their power with a council.

New York City mayor Bill de Blasio spoke to reporters about new city legislation in 2016.

Local governments are important. They include people from the places they serve. These people know the needs of the residents. Local authority is limited. All towns, cities, and counties must follow federal laws. They must follow the laws of their state, too. No local laws can conflict with federal or state laws.

The federal government was created to treat Americans equally. All citizens obey the same national laws. They have the same rights under the law. However, Americans live in a variety of places. The federal government is not always able to meet the needs of people or communities. That's when state and local authorities step in. The state, local, and national governments work together.

GLOSSARY

advisers (ad-VYE-zerz) Advisers help others by giving them advice. The president's advisers are experts on different subjects.

citizens (SIT-uh-zunz) Citizens are people who live in a certain nation and are given certain rights. Governments are made to protect their citizens.

constitution (kon-sti-TOO-shun) A constitution explains the basic laws of a nation. The constitution of the United States established a national government.

democracy (di-MOK-ruh-see) A democracy is a government run by the people. The United States is a democracy.

diplomats (DIP-luh-mats) Diplomats are government officials who represent the nation overseas. Diplomats might meet with foreign leaders.

federal (FED-er-ul) The federal government is the national government. The president is the head of the federal government.

federalism (FED-er-uh-liz-um) Federalism means shared power between the national and state governments. Federalism is a key idea of the U.S. government.

issue (ISH-oo) To issue is to give or deliver something. State governments issue driver's licenses to residents.

legislature (LEJ-is-ley-chur) A legislature is a group of people who meet and make laws for a nation. Congress is the U.S. legislature.

parliament (PAR-luh-munt) Parliament is the name of the legislature in many countries. In some ways, the U.S. government was like Britain's parliament.

representatives (rep-ri-ZEN-tuh-tivz) Representatives are people who can represent or speak for others. Government representatives might support laws to help their community.

seceded (si-SEED-id) When something has seceded, it has stopped being part of a group or union. During the Civil War, 11 states seceded from the United States.

veto (VEE-toh) To veto means to reject. The president can veto bills passed by Congress.

TO LEARN MORE

IN THE LIBRARY

Burgan, Michael. *The Branches of U.S. Government.*
New York: Children's Press, 2012.

Sobel, Syl. *How the U.S. Government Works.* Hauppauge, NY: Barron's, 2012.

Thomas, William. *What Are the Parts of
Government?* Pleasantville, NY: Gareth Stevens, 2008.

ON THE WEB

Visit our Web site for links about how
the government works: **childsworld.com/links**

Note to Parents, Teachers, and Librarians: We routinely verify our Web links to make
sure they are safe and active sites. So encourage your readers to check them out!

INDEX

ABOUT THE AUTHOR

Jeanne Marie Ford is an Emmy-winning television scriptwriter and holds a master of fine arts degree in writing for children from Vermont College. She has written numerous children's books and articles. Ford also teaches college English. She lives in Maryland with her husband and two children.